FROM PLANT
To Blue Jeans

A Photo Essay
by Arthur John L'Hommedieu

Children's Press

A Division of Grolier Publishing
New York London Hong Kong Sydney
Danbury, Connecticut

Created and Developed by the Learning Source
Designed by Josh Simons

Acknowledgments: The Learning Source would like to thank the National Cotton Council of America, Cone Mills Corporation, and Wrangler, Inc., for their help. Without their cooperation and assistance this book would not have been possible. Very special thanks goes to Kellie K. Clark at Wrangler Inc. for all her efforts on our behalf.

Photo Credits: Norvia Behling/Behling & Johnson Photography: 7 (left); Cone Mills Corporation: 17, 19, 20; Russel A. Graves: 4; Ken Karp: 3, 5, 6, 7 (right); Bertram T. Knight/The Learning Source: 32 (right bottom); Arthur John L'Hommedieu/The Learning Source: 32 (left top, right top, and right center); National Cotton Council of America: front cover, 2, 8, 9, 10, 11, 12, 13, 14, 15, 16; Lynn M. Stone: 29; Jim Stratford/Cone Mills Corporation: 18, 21; SuperStock Inc.: 28, 30, 31; Wrangler Inc.: 22, 23, 24, 25, 26, 27, 32 (left center and left bottom).

Note: The actual jeans-making process often varies from manufacturer to manufacturer. The facts and details included in this book are representative of one way of producing jeans today.

Library of Congress Cataloging-in-Publication Data
L'Hommedieu, Arthur John.
        From plant to blue jeans : a photo essay by Arthur J. L'Hommedieu.
              p.   cm. — (Changes)
        Includes Index.
        Summary: Describes the process of making blue jeans from the harvesting of cotton through the weaving of cloth and sewing the finished product.
        ISBN 0-516-20738-5 (lib. bdg.) 0-516-20366-5 (pbk.)
        1. Jeans (Clothing)—Juvenile literature. 2. Cotton fabrics—Juvenile literature. 3. Cotton manufacturing—Juvenile literature. [1. Jeans (Clothing) 2. Cotton.] I. Title. II. Series: Changes (New York, N.Y.)
TT605.L46   1997
687'.1—dc21   97-23610 CIP
                                   AC
Printed in the United States of America
1 2 3 4 5 6 7 8 9 10 R 05 05 04 03 02 01 00 99 98 97

3

Levi Strauss invented blue jeans about 150 years ago.
Since then, these tough pants have been worn by all
sorts of people . . .

. . . doing all kinds of things . . .

. . . in many different places.

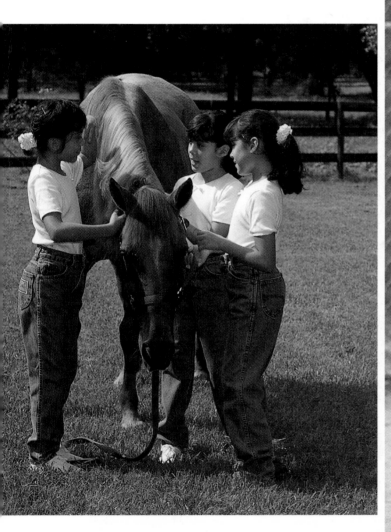

But how are blue jeans made?

They begin on a cotton farm where . . .

. . . special machines plant cotton seeds, many rows at a time.

In a month or so, small white flowers form on the little cotton plants.

Three days later the flowers change color and die.
They leave behind tiny pods called cotton bolls.

The bolls grow and ripen. Finally they open, showing seeds and fluffy cotton within.

At harvest time, machines pick the white cotton from the bolls, seeds and all.

The raw cotton is pressed into huge rectangles . . .

. . . and taken to the cotton gin. Here, the soft cotton is separated from its hard seeds.

The cotton comes out of the gin in bales shaped like these. The bales go to the textile mill where . . .

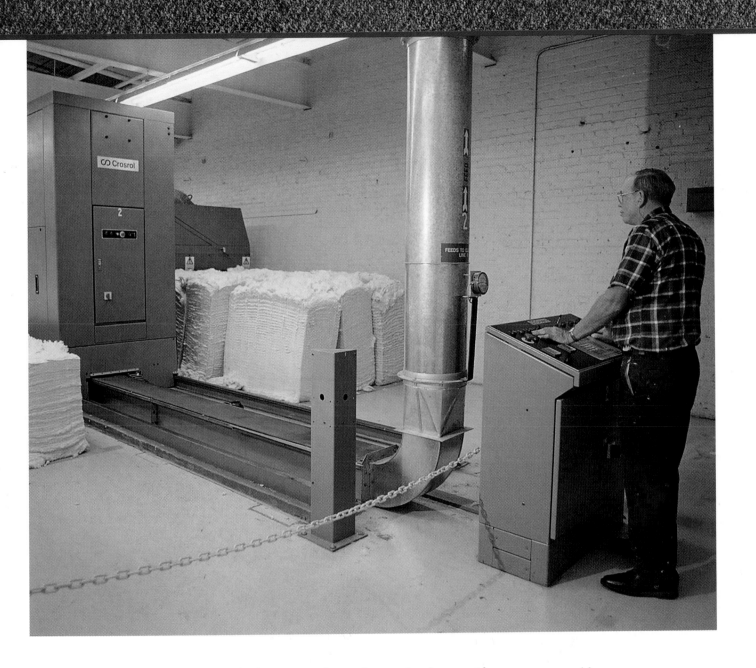

. . . machines unload and clean the raw cotton.

The clean cotton fibers are gathered together, pulled, and stretched. Finally, they are twisted into thin strands of yarn.

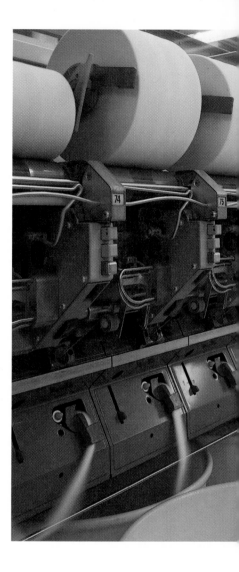

Some of the yarn stays its natural white color. The rest is dyed a deep indigo blue.

The yarn is wound onto spools. Blue yarn (called warp) will become the outside of your jeans. White yarn (called filler) will become the light-colored inside.

This machine weaves the blue and white yarns into denim fabric. Spool after spool intertwine as the denim winds onto huge rolls.

At the jeans factory, a forklift carries denim to the spreading table. There, up to 60 pairs of jeans are cut out at one time.

Then the jeans are sewn up in stages—all by machine. One operator sews left and right sides together. Another sews fronts to backs. This person is sewing the seat and . . .

. . . this person is doing the waist. The jeans are taking shape. They have pockets, belt loops, and zippers.

One of the last steps is sewing the bottom hems. The jeans are then tagged and labeled.

Some are washed, dried, and pressed for a softer look and feel.

Finally, an inspector checks for flaws. Then the jeans go to the warehouse and out to stores near you.

Blue jeans—wear them for reaching to the sky . . .

. . . or coming down to earth . . .

. . . or hanging out with friends . . .

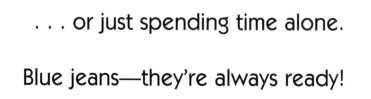

. . . or just spending time alone.

Blue jeans—they're always ready!

Denim is not just for jeans.
Which of these denim items have you seen?

Laundry Bag

Jacket

Shirt

Overalls

Shorts

Shoes